GREAT MYSTERIES

Edited by Caroline Clayton and Damian Kelleher

Written by Robert Nicholson

WORLD BOOK / TWO-CAN

GREAT MYSTERIES

This edition published in
the United States in 1997
by World Book Inc.
525 W. Monroe
Chicago, IL 60661
in association with
Two-Can Publishing Ltd.

**For information on other World Book products,
call 1-800-255-1750, x 2238.**

ISBN: 0-7166-4505-X

Printed in Hong Kong

1 2 3 4 5 6 7 8 9 10 99 98 97 96

Design by Elizabeth Bell. Art directed by Catherine Page. Picture research by Debbie Dorman. Production by Lis Clegg.

Picture credits:
Fortean Picture Library: 5, 8/9, 10 (Rene Dahinden), 19tr (PUFORG) cr (Philip Panton), br (Rene Dahinden), 24/25; Aerofilms 12/13; Britstock-Ifa/JAY 14; South American Pictures/Tony Morrison 16/17; Mary Evans 18/19c, 19tl & cl, 26t, 30b; Popperfoto 19bl; Griffith Institute/Ashmolean Museum 20; World Pictures 21t; Bridgeman Art Library/Giraudon 21b, Syndication Int. 22; Ronald Grant Archive 23t; Ardea/Francois Gohier 27; Leeds University 30t, 31; Robert Harding: front cover main photo.

Illustrations:
Oliver Frey 4/5, 6/7, 9, 10, 15, 16/17, 28; Maureen & Gordon Gray 11, 29; John James 20/21; Barry Mitchell 22, 27; Chris West 23; Bernard Long 24, 26b; Woody 31. Lettering: John Aldritch.

CONTENTS

LOCH NESS IN SCOTLAND IS HUGE, 1,000 ft DEEP IN PLACES, 24 MILES LONG, AND OFTEN A MILE WIDE.

BUT IS IT HOME TO A HUGE MONSTER?

St. COLUMBA VISITED LOCH NESS IN AD 565 AND, SO THE STORY GOES, ONE OF HIS COMPANIONS WAS ATTACKED BY A MONSTER.

GO BACK, FOUL MONSTER!

THANK THE LORD, COLUMBA. YOU'VE MADE IT TURN AWAY.

THIS WAS THE FIRST OF MANY "SIGHTINGS."

In the past, practical jokers have played tricks on Nessie-watchers. In 1977, two schoolboys fooled a cameraman into believing that he had captured the monster moving on film.

SS MONSTER

monster hoax? It's up to you to decide

The Loch Ness Monster is a huge creature that some people believe lives deep in Loch Ness, a lake in northern Scotland.

Hundreds claim to have seen the animal, which is nicknamed Nessie. The monster is said to measure up to 30 feet in length. It is thought to have flippers, one or two humps, and a long, thin neck. Is Nessie a plesiosaur, a marine reptile believed to have become extinct with the dinosaurs about 65 million years ago?

In the 1930s a new road was built to the loch, giving more people access to its shores. After this, there were even more sightings of Nessie reported.

NESSIE OR NOT NESSIE?

In 1960, the BBC broadcast a program about the Loch Ness Monster. Many people claimed that the footage shown on the program proved that Nessie really did exist.

The Loch Ness Monster has been given the scientific name Nessiteras rhombopteryx so it can be protected by a British law that safeguards rare animals.

Once again, people flocked to the lake, and soon afterward the Loch Ness Investigation Bureau (or LNIB) was set up. LNIB scientists went to Loch Ness with some sophisticated underwater equipment to try to solve the case once and for all. Investigations with sonar, a device that uses sound to detect underwater objects, have found that there are large, moving bodies in Loch Ness.

But experts can't agree on exactly what the findings prove, so the monster mystery continues. Meanwhile, all over the world, tales abound of other mysterious monsters lurking in rivers, lakes, and seas.

▶ In 1934 a national newspaper published one of the first photographs of Nessie. However, 60 years later, this photograph was revealed as a hoax.

L och Ness isn't the only place in the world with a monster mystery. In North America alone there are more than 100 lakes where all kinds of mythical monsters have been spotted. Some of them resemble extinct dinosaurs and others look like strange, crossbred creatures.

Others still are said to look like real animals, only much bigger. One, known as the Beast of 'Busco, is said to be a giant, fish-gobbling turtle that some eyewitnesses claim is the size of a pickup truck. The people of Churubusco, Indiana, where the monster lives, have nicknamed it Oscar!

MONSTER MYTHS

But where is the proof? Despite thousands of sightings, no one has ever found the body of a dead monster or even the remains of its bones. Hundreds of photographs have been taken, yet none provides certain proof of a real-life monster.

THE MONSTER DETECTIVES

Cryptozoology is the scientific study of animals that are not recognized or accepted by other scientists. Cryptozoologists pick a particular animal and try to prove it exists by finding bones, taking pictures, or even capturing a live example if they're lucky!

Many animals have been discovered by scientists only in the last 150 years. The coelacanth is a fish that was thought to have become extinct 60 or 70 million years ago (at the same time as dinosaurs). But in 1938 some African fishermen caught one in the Indian Ocean.

Since then, several others have been fished out of the sea and studied. Surely there must be more "extinct" animals just waiting to be discovered.

▲ FREAKY FAMILY

A monster named Manipogo is said to live in Lake Manitoba in Canada. Local people claim to have seen monsters in the lake for hundreds of years. In 1960, three beasts were spotted together – a monster family of mother, father, and baby!

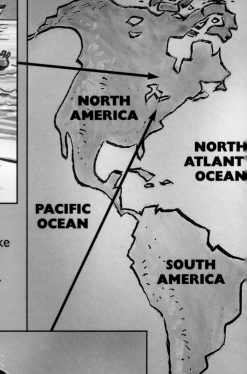

NORTH AMERICA

NORTH ATLANT OCEAN

PACIFIC OCEAN

SOUTH AMERICA

▲ HE IS THE CHAMP!

In the depths of Lake Champlain, on the border of New York State and Canada, lurks a monstrous creature affectionately known as Champ.

The lake is 101 miles long and nearly 330 feet deep – big enough for a monster to make its home. First spotted in 1609, Champ was finally photographed in 1977. He's said to be nearly 33 feet long with the head of a huge horse. Neigh!

F THE DEEP

live in this monster of a map

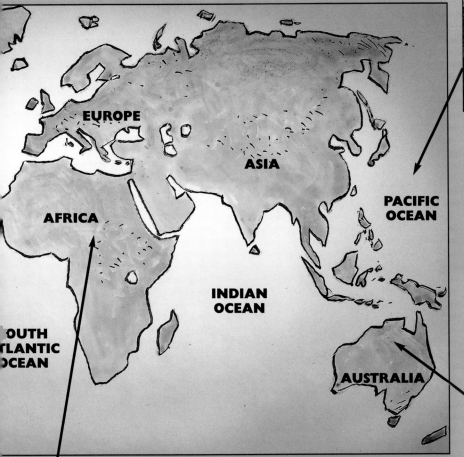

EUROPE

ASIA

AFRICA

PACIFIC
OCEAN

INDIAN
OCEAN

OUTH
TLANTIC
OCEAN

AUSTRALIA

▲ SQUIDS ALIVE!

In the 1930s, a 160,000-ton tanker called the *Brunswick* was attacked by a giant squid. Eventually, the monster was chopped to pieces by the ship's propellers. Sixty-six-foot specimens have been recorded in the past, and some cryptozoologists claim that huge 165-200-foot monster squid lurk deep in the tropical oceans.

◀ REWARD – $2,000!

Mokele-Mbembe is a large reptile said to live in the swamps of Central Africa. It was first reported some 200 years ago and takes its name from a word meaning "he who stops the flow of rivers." Could Mokele-Mbembe be a type of dinosaur that has survived from the Cretaceous era, 65 million years ago? There is a $2,000 reward for anyone who can produce evidence of its existence.

▲ SPOTTED!

Aboriginal people in Australia tell stories of a giant monster they call Bunyip. In the early 19th century, an escaped convict named William Buckley claimed he saw one the size of a huge dog, complete with fins for swimming.

If you go into the woods today, you're in for a big hairy surprise!

Big Hairy Monsters, or BHMs as they are called, have been sighted all over the world. From the west coast of the United States and Canada, through China, Mongolia, Russia, and the Himalayas, there are thousands of eye-witness reports of hairy man-ape beasts. But what are these creatures? Can we prove they exist?

BHMs are usually between five and eight feet tall and covered with thick black or reddish-brown hair. A typical BHM looks like a cross between a human being and an ape, or like a primitive human.

A BHM BY ANY OTHER NAME...

North America *Sasquatch* (Native American name), *Bigfoot*

Himalayas *Metoh-Kangmi* (Tibetan for "abominable snowman"), *Yeti* (Tibetan for "mountain creature" or "spirit")

China *Yeren*

Mongolia and Urals *Alma*

Australia *Yowie* (Aboriginal name)

HORRIBLE AND *Hairy!*

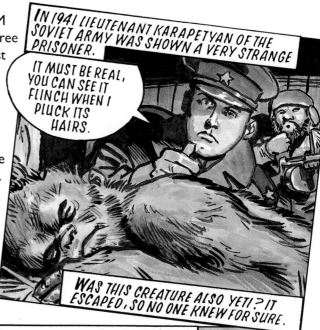

MONSTER MEETINGS

There's one thing all BHM witnesses agree upon. Almost everyone who has come close to a BHM says the creatures are really smelly. So if you go on a Yeti hunt, don't forget the clothes pin for your nose!

IN 1941 LIEUTENANT KARAPETYAN OF THE SOVIET ARMY WAS SHOWN A VERY STRANGE PRISONER.

IT MUST BE REAL, YOU CAN SEE IT FLINCH WHEN I PLUCK ITS HAIRS.

WAS THIS CREATURE ALSO YETI? IT ESCAPED, SO NO ONE KNEW FOR SURE.

IN 1979 A SHERPA FRIGHTENED AWAY A BHM WITH A STICK...

GET OUT OF HERE, YOU HORRIBLE CREATURE.

LATER FRENCH SCIENTISTS EXAMINED SOME HAIRS FROM THE END OF THE STICK — AND DISCOVERED THEY CAME FROM AN **UNKNOWN** PRIMATE!

THOUSANDS OF BIGFOOT SIGHTINGS HAVE BEEN REPORTED, BUT MANY ARE HOAXES...

YOU TERRIFIED PEOPLE WITH YOUR BIGFOOT COSTUME. I'M FINING YOU $100.

▲ In 1967, ace monster-tracker Roger Patterson managed to film a Bigfoot. These are still photos from his film. Scientific experts who analyzed the film were astounded and could not decide whether it showed a real BHM or a tall man in a hairy suit.

"I couldn't see the zipper, and I still can't," said John Napier of the Smithsonian Institute.

FOOT NOTES

Do the huge footprint photos prove that the incredible Yeti really does exist?

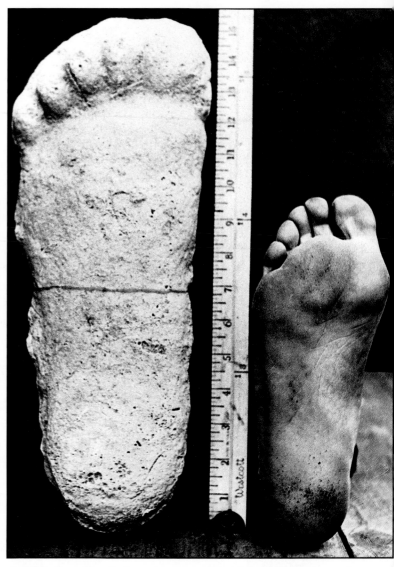

▲ *This is one of the pictures that Eric Shipton took on his 1951 expedition. It sparked off scores of Yeti hunts in the Himalayas.*

THE CAMERA NEVER LIES!

IN 1951 ERIC SHIPTON, A BRITISH MOUNTAINEER, ARRIVED BACK FROM THE HIMALAYAS.

I HAVE SOME AMAZING PICTURES HERE OF HUGE, STRANGE FOOTPRINTS.

DID SHIPTON HAVE THE EVIDENCE THAT PROVED THE EXISTENCE OF BHMs?

★ Or does it? Some BHM tracks have been photographed in the United States and in the Himalayas. They seem to indicate that the BHM prints are nothing like an ape's. For a start, apes' feet have a thumb, which is certainly not visible in BHM tracks. Photographs of BHMs and their footprints can be misleading. The repeated melting and freezing of prints left in snow can greatly alter their shape and size. Many photos of BHMs are blurred and very faint. And some have been proven to be fakes.

YETI OR BIGFOOT – WHATEVER YOU CALL IT, DOES IT EXIST?

UGH! URGH!

LAND OF THE GIANTS

★ Other theories suggest that BHMs are survivors of the species *Giantopithecus*. This was a giant ape that lived in China and was thought to have become extinct 300,000 years ago. Giantopithecus could have crossed the Bering Strait into America, exactly as the American Indians and Eskimos did, about 12,000 years ago.

IS THIS ANOTHER SHIP LOST IN THE TRIANGLE?

THE **BERMUDA TRIANGLE** A Mystery of

Briton lost in Bermuda Triangle

By Paul Stokes

BERMUDA

FLORIDA

THE BAHAMAS

ATLANTIC OCEAN

PUERTO RICO

THREE-SIDED MYSTERY
The Bermuda Triangle covers an area of roughly 440,000 square miles. That's some triangle!

VANISHING POINT

What terrible secret lies within the Bermuda Triangle?

Off the southeast coast of the United States, there lies an area of the Atlantic Ocean known as the Bermuda Triangle. Within this zone, more than 50 ships and planes have disappeared under mysterious circumstances during this century. What's especially puzzling is that few captains or pilots have sent radio distress messages before they vanished forever.

WHAT'S GOING ON?

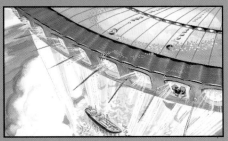

★ Nobody knows for sure what causes these strange disappearances. Some scientists claim that sudden shifts in the earth's magnetic field in the area may be to blame. Or perhaps downward air currents are the key to the mystery. And some even believe that UFO's and aliens are the cause of all the problems. Beam me up, Scotty!

The first recorded disappearance took place in 1918 when the U.S.S. *Cyclops* vanished while sailing through the area. Then in 1945, a squadron of five U.S. bomber planes disappeared without a trace near the Bahamas. The Navy sent out a search plane to investigate, but that, too, failed to return.

OUT OF FUEL? OUT OF LUCK?

What could have happened to the missing planes? All the pilots in the squadron were trainees, and it's possible that they simply lost their way and ran out of fuel. As for the search plane, some witnesses claim to have seen an explosion over the area. This could have been the plane blowing up. After all, this particular aircraft was known by pilots as "the Flying Gas Tank."

NEW-FANGLED ANGLE

In 1964, a journalist named Vincent Gaddis published a book about the area. This was the first time that the phrase "Bermuda Triangle" was used and it created a huge stir. Soon, accounts of other disappearances within the area came flooding in – as they still do today.

MONUMEN

TAL MYSTERY

There's nothing plain about the stunning Stone Age spectacle in Wiltshire, England

Two hundred years before the Egyptians built the Great Pyramids, Stone Age Britons began work on a huge circle of rocks. But just why is still a mystery.

Stone circles were built in Europe from about 3000 to 1200 B.C. There are more than 900 in Great Britain alone, and Stonehenge, on Salisbury Plain in Wiltshire, is perhaps the greatest of them all.

MUSCLE MEN

Its construction is a mind-boggling feat. How Stonehenge was built is an engineering mystery – the Stone Age Britons who built it had no iron tools for digging and carving. And at that time, they didn't even have the wheel to help them drag the huge stones around.

Hundreds of men would have toiled long and hard to create Britain's best-known prehistoric monument. The upright stones (called sarsens) in the outer circle came from the Marlborough Downs, over 18 miles away. And it's thought that the sandstones standing upright in the inner circle came from Pembrokeshire in Wales. That's over 120 miles away! Imagine the effort of dragging stones weighing up to four tons each over sea and land. More than 600 men would have been needed to pull each stone!

In 1988, a sandstone was found on the bed of the Daugleddau River at Llsngwm in Wales. It is a similar size and shape to those of Stonehenge and experts believe it fell off its raft during the journey.

SECRET OF THE STONES

But the real mystery of the monument is its purpose. What was it used for? It might have been a religious center where ceremonies were held and sacrifices made. Some experts believe it was some kind of astronomical observatory used for studying the sun, moon, and stars.

Whatever the answer, it must have been important to the ancient people who built it. After all, researchers estimate it would have taken millions of hours and hundreds of years to complete.

THE SPHINX

Can you solve the puzzle behind the guardian of the pyramids?

At Giza, Egypt, a strange statue stands guard over the tombs of the pharaohs. With the head of a human and the body of a lion, the fearsome beast was meant to keep robbers away from the precious pyramids.

ROCK SOLID
It's hard to believe that the incredible sphinx was built about 4,500 years ago. The whole of the impressive statue at Giza, except for its legs and paws, is carved from one single piece of rock. At this time, the Egyptians often sculpted sphinxes to honor a king or queen.

In full, this sphinx measures 66 feet high and 240 feet long. Its face is over 13 feet wide. The face was modeled after Khafre, one of the pharaohs of Egypt.

TELL ME A RIDDLE
The sphinx is found in many cultures, not just in that of ancient Egypt. In Greek mythology, for example, it has the body of a lion, the head of a woman, a pair of wings, and a serpent's tail. According to Greek legend, the Sphinx asked everyone who saw her a riddle. The punishment for getting the answer wrong was instant death.

"What animal, goes on four feet in the morning, two at midday, and three in the evening?" Can you figure it out for yourself?

PROBLEM SOLVED
Finally, a Greek prince named Oedipus gave the Sphinx the correct answer. It was "a man." When he is a baby, man crawls on all fours. Then as he grows, he walks on two legs. Finally, as an old man, he leans on a cane – the "third foot" of the riddle.

The Sphinx was so furious that someone had finally solved her riddle that she jumped to her death from the high rock on which she lived.

WHAT A BEAST!
A roundup of some other creepy mythical creatures – part human, part animal

Griffin
Griffins (above) had the head and wings of an eagle, the body of a lion, and the tail of a snake. They were very greedy and loved feasting upon people and horses!

Unicorn
The unicorn was like a horse with a single horn in the middle of its head. It was probably based on the rhinoceros.

Centaur
Centaurs had a horse's body and the head and shoulders of a man. They loved whooping it up and spent most of their time getting drunk. Hic!

Minotaur
This infamous monster (below) lived in the labyrinth below the palace of King Minos of Crete. Part bull and part man, the beast was fed seven maidens and seven youths every nine years, until Theseus of Athens finally killed it in an epic struggle.

Back in the 16th century, when Spanish explorers first arrived in South America, there was talk of a fabulously rich native Indian king named El Dorado – the Golden Man.

He is said to have lived in a beautiful city, hidden deep in the jungle, where the streets were paved with gold.

PRECIOUS DUST

Legend has it that once a year a ceremony was held to show the power and wealth of the king. He was covered in clay and then sprinkled all over with gold dust. Amid music and singing he was taken to the center of a lake on a raft, where he dived in and then emerged, the gold now washed off and sinking to the bottom.

Explorers from Europe flocked to what is now Colombia to find the lake, the city, and the gold. For centuries, prospectors have searched for the legendary golden city of El Dorado, but it remains undiscovered.

THE GOLDEN LAKE

Lake Guatavita, in Colombia, sits 9,000 feet above sea level in the crater of an extinct volcano. In 1540, Spanish treasure-seeker Hernán Perez de Quesada spent three unsuccessful months trying

▲ Is the legend of El Dorado – the Golden Man – true?

to drain the lake dry. He believed this was where El Dorado had bathed and left his gold behind.

Another attempt to drain the lake began in 1580, but only one emerald and a few gold trinkets were found by the Colombian merchant behind this ill-fated venture. Then, in 1912, the lake was drained completely, revealing precious little gold. What was removed was valued at roughly one tenth of the cost of the whole project – certainly not worth the effort!

▲ Is Lake Guatavit

LOST CITY
What became of El Dorado, the legendary golden city of South America?

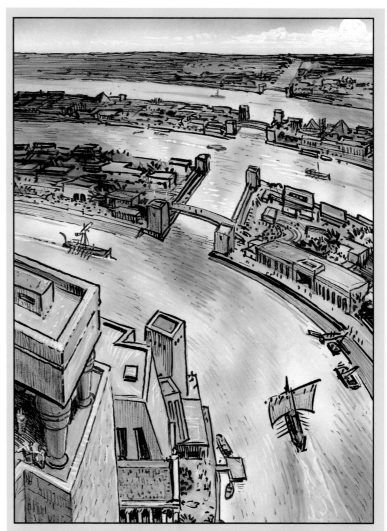

▲ *The city of Atlantis could have looked like this.*

LOST AND FOUND

★ Legend has it that, thousands of years ago, there was a wealthy and highly advanced civilization on an island called Atlantis. Volcanic eruptions destroyed the city and it sank beneath a massive tidal wave, lost forever.

Earlier this century, an American psychic named Edgar Cayce claimed he had visited Atlantis in a trance. He said its people had developed X rays and televisions, and he pinpointed Bimini, in the Bahamas, as the site. He also predicted that part of the city would be revealed in 1968. Amazingly, two divers did discover huge parallel lines of stones under the sea off the coast of Bimini that very year. Was this the lost city of Atlantis?

TROJAN TROVE

For hundreds of years, the city of Troy was considered nothing more than a legend. Then, in 1873, German archaeologist Heinrich Schliemann discovered the city walls in northern Turkey and proved its existence. Maybe it won't be long before experts find conclusive proof of Atlantis's existence too, and the history books will have to be rewritten.

...den wonder? Apparently not!

UFO'S

No, it isn't a bird and it isn't a plane. So what are the strange shapes that have been spotted in our skies?

Unidentified Flying Objects (UFO's) first hit the headlines way back in 1947.

Businessman Kenneth Arnold was flying over the Cascade Mountains in the United States when he saw what looked like nine circular, metallic objects. They were flying in formation at great speed, weaving in and out of the mountain peaks. They didn't look like planes and Arnold described them as "a chain of saucer-like things."

Soon reports of "flying saucers" were flooding in from all over the world. Now, nearly 50 years later, an average of about 40 sightings are reported every day.

BALLS OF CONFUSION

So what exactly is a UFO? Without a doubt, some of the sightings are hoaxes. Then again, some are probably illusions created by atmospheric conditions – cloud formations or ball lightning – while others may be high-altitude weather balloons or satellites breaking up on reentry to the atmosphere.

But that still leaves other sightings that can't be explained away. Could these be visits by alien beings from outer space? Check out these reported sightings and decide for yourself!

● The cigar-shaped UFO that a jazz band saw in Glasgow, Scotland, in 1955 fits the exact description of one that visited Manchester, England in 1982. Did the UFO come back for a second look at our planet?

● U.S. Air Force pilot Thomas Mantell saw a huge, metallic UFO in 1948. He chased it high into the sky before his own plane came crashing inexplicably back down to Earth.

TOO CLOSE FOR COMFORT

UFOlogists divide UFO incidents into three kinds of close encounters:

1 Close encounters of the first kind (CE1) are classed as UFO sightings.

2 Close encounters of the second kind (CE2) are sightings and permanent evidence, such as marks in the ground or burns on grass.

3 Close encounters of the third kind (CE3) are actual contacts with alien beings from a UFO.

▲ Saucers over Sicily: Several witnesses spotted these UFO's back in 1954.

PROOF POSITIVE?

These photos are "evidence" of famous UFO sightings. But are they real or fake? It's up to you to decide!

▲This flying saucer zoomed into Paul Trent's viewfinder one evening in Oregon.

▲ Ignore the giraffe – what's that strange object to the left? Just another tall tale, perhaps?

▲ These disks put several quarry workers in a quandary in Larchant, France.

▲ It came from anywhere but outer space. These spheres are definite fakes!

▲ Looks like a lampshade? Well, it's Adamski's flying saucer, photographed in 1952.

▲ Cosmic clouds at Mount Shasta – or visitors from another planet?

WHOOPS!
The planet Venus is called "the Queen of the UFO's" because it's been mistaken for one so many times!

Did a dreadful fate await the discoverers of King Tut's tomb?

In 1917, an English archaeologist named Howard Carter began excavations in the Valley of the Kings. His aim was to find the tomb of the boy king, Tutankhamen, who died in 1339 B.C. when he was just eighteen.

Carter's search was funded by Lord Caernarvon, a wealthy aristocrat. But by 1922, money was running out and it looked as though the whole quest would have to be called off.

HIDDEN ENTRANCE

Then, on November 26, 1922, Carter and Caernarvon discovered the entrance to Tutankhamen's tomb. It had been hidden under debris thrown up by a dig at another tomb in the valley.

Egyptian workers helping Carter and Caernarvon were very superstitious about the discovery. They believed that the lucky pair had found the tomb largely thanks to the pet canary that Howard Carter had bought recently.

Shortly after the discovery, James Bresred, an American archaeologist, heard a loud "almost human" cry from behind Carter's quarters. The canary had been killed by a king cobra, a creature that was often used to represent Tutankhamen himself.

Immediately, there was talk of a curse on the tomb and of terrible fates that would befall those who had opened it.

Within weeks, Lord Caernarvon was dead after an insect bite became infected. He was just 53. At the very moment when he died, all the lights in Cairo went out for no reason at all. Back home, his trusty dog let out a terrible howl and collapsed – dead.

GET CARTER

Two more victims of the "curse" followed shortly thereafter. George Bendite, an archaeologist, and Arthur Mace, a friend of Carter, both died suddenly after visiting the site. By now, rumors of a curse were spreading fast.

Yet the one person who remained untouched by the curse was Carter himself.

He spent a further 10 years clearing and cataloging the contents of the amazing tomb – a considerable task. Eventually, he died of natural causes in 1939.

CURSE CONTINUES

In 1962, Dr. Ezzedin Taha thought he had solved the mystery of Tutankhamen's dreaded curse once and for all. He claimed the numerous deaths that had followed the opening of the tomb could all be traced back to one cause – deadly bacteria.

Dr. Taha's theory stated that dangerous, disease-carrying bacteria had been sealed into the tomb along with the boy king and his glittering prizes. So when the tomb was reopened, its innocent discoverers walked straight into a fatal trap.

Alas, Dr. Taha never had the chance to conduct further research to prove his theory. Just days after explaining away the catastrophic curse to the world, he too died – in a mysterious car crash.

▲ 3,000 years old and still a boy!

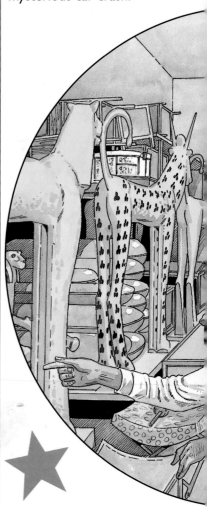

E MUMMY

FIND OF THE CENTURY

THIS IS MADE OF SOLID GOLD!

AND EVERYTHING IS PERFECTLY PRESERVED!

▲ This solid gold mask showing the young king's face covered the head and shoulders of Tutankhamen's mummy. It is thought to show him as the sun-god.

★ Howard Carter (left) and Lord Caernarvon (right) are the names behind the most exciting archaeological discovery this century.

"Can you see anything?" Caernarvon asked Carter. "Yes, wonderful things!" Carter replied. And he was right. Inside the tomb were all kinds of beautiful items, including trumpets, thrones, and several statues of the boy king himself.

Most other pharaohs' tombs had been plundered by robbers hundreds of years before. But apart from a side room, which had been disturbed, Tutankhamen's treasures were found exactly as they had been left more than 32 centuries before!

EGYPTIAN AFTERLIFE

The Egyptians were firm believers in life after death. To prepare them for the next world, they mummified (embalmed and dried) corpses to prevent the bodies from decaying. People were usually buried with their favorite possessions and objects that would be of practical use to them in the afterlife.

The Egyptians also believed that jewelry was a lucky charm against danger. Favorite pieces like this scarab brooch (below) found in Tut's chamber were placed with them in the tombs, but some were also specially made to fit the mummy.

At the funeral, a priest would touch the mummy's mouth, hands, and feet so that the spirit could enter the body in the afterlife. Then it was ready to breathe again.

MIND OVER MATTER

Is Uri Geller the greatest modern magician or a mind-bending psychic?

Uri Geller has bent forks and spoons, fixed broken watches, and read people's minds all over the world.

Born in Tel Aviv in 1946, Geller appeared on British television on November 23, 1973, when he bent a fork by stroking it gently with his fingers. Hundreds of viewers called the BBC to say that they too had bent forks while watching him. Gellermania swept the country.

Some skeptics claimed that he used force, so a device to measure pressure was rigged up to the brass strip he was rubbing. It showed just half an ounce of pressure – not nearly enough to bend metal.

TRICK OR TREAT
Experts at the Stanford Research Institute in California could find no trace of fakery or trickery. However, a magician named James Randi has fooled scientists by bending cutlery using magic tricks.

Is Uri Geller the smartest magician ever or does he really have incredible psychic powers? A number of scientists have tried to show that he is a fake, but no one has ever been able to prove it.

▲ *Uri doesn't use force to bend steel cutlery – he just strokes them gently.*

Are these amazing winged relatives of the dinosaurs still alive and well?

Eighty million years ago, the pterosaur ruled the airways. Undisputed king of the skies, this massive, flying reptile had a wingspan of up to 36 feet. Although it is thought that the pterosaur died out with the rest of its dino cousins, there have been reports of similar winged beasts sighted in recent times.

In 1933, two British Museum scientists saw a giant, batlike creature flying over a river in Cameroon. As large as a huge eagle, local tribesmen called it an Olitiau. Similar creatures have also been seen in Zimbabwe, Namibia, Zambia, and the Sierra Madre mountains in Mexico.

BATTY BIRD

In Java, legends abound of the Athol, a giant fur-covered, batlike bird with the face of a monkey. The creature is said to be named after its long, howling call (aah-ooool). Those who have seen the Athol talk of its weird, turned-back feet. Dr. Ernest Bartels, who has

▲ *Pterosaurs dominated the skies for almost as long as dinosaurs ruled the earth.*

LIVING LEGENDS

himself spotted the Athol, is convinced it is actually a species of giant bat, rather than a survivor of the dinosaur era. After all, bats' feet do point backward — and their funny-looking faces are very similar to those of monkeys.

If the pterosaur has survived from the age of the dinosaurs, it does raise some very important questions. To begin with, how could such a massive creature hide away for so long? And how on earth did it manage to survive throughout the centuries?

SWOOP SCOOP

★ The thunderbird is a giant bird in Native American mythology, based on a condor or eagle. In 1886, hunters killed an enormous bird and measured its wingspan. Six men, standing fingertip to fingertip, could only just stretch from the tip of one wing to the other – a distance of about 33 feet!

A plane that crashed in Maryland in 1962 was found to be covered with blood and birds' feathers. Officials said it had flown into a flock of geese. But could geese have made the huge gouge marks on its fuselage? Or was it brought down by a giant thunderbird?

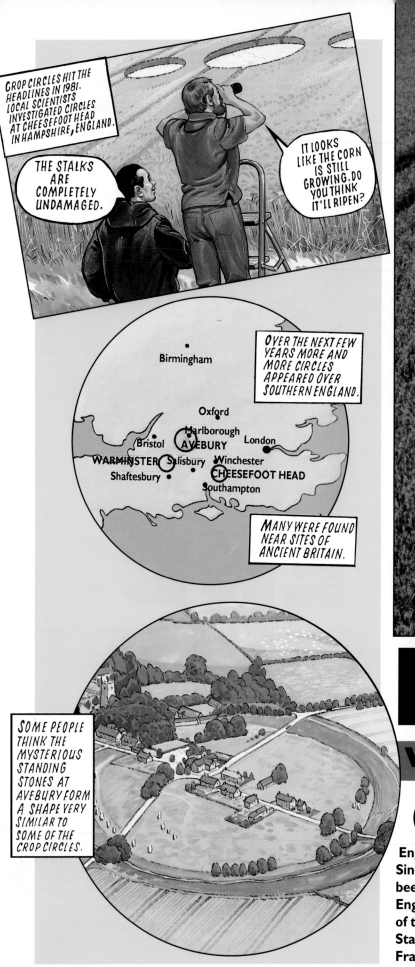

CROP CIRCLES HIT THE HEADLINES IN 1981. LOCAL SCIENTISTS INVESTIGATED CIRCLES AT CHEESEFOOT HEAD IN HAMPSHIRE, ENGLAND.

THE STALKS ARE COMPLETELY UNDAMAGED.

IT LOOKS LIKE THE CORN IS STILL GROWING. DO YOU THINK IT'LL RIPEN?

OVER THE NEXT FEW YEARS MORE AND MORE CIRCLES APPEARED OVER SOUTHERN ENGLAND.

Birmingham

Oxford

Marlborough

Bristol AVEBURY London

WARMINSTER Salisbury Winchester

Shaftesbury CHEESEFOOT HEAD

Southampton

MANY WERE FOUND NEAR SITES OF ANCIENT BRITAIN.

SOME PEOPLE THINK THE MYSTERIOUS STANDING STONES AT AVEBURY FORM A SHAPE VERY SIMILAR TO SOME OF THE CROP CIRCLES.

MAGIC

What makes these strange

Crop circles were first officially recorded in England in the 19th century. Since then, several have been found all over southern England and in other parts of the world – the United States, Brazil, Australia, France, and Russia.

They are often formed in fantastic and beautiful shapes. Circles make up the basic pattern, but there have also been ringed circles, spoked wheels, rectangles, and straight lines. More complex pictograms have also been found in the shape of dolphins, stars, or even

CIRCLES

wirling patterns in the countryside?

KEY TO A MYSTERY?

★ In July 1990, one of the most wonderful crop configurations ever appeared at Alton Barnes in the Vale of Pewsey in Wiltshire, England. Over 250 feet long, this was the first in a series of "double pictograms" and boasted ringed circles with "satellites" at the top of the formation. These circles have distinctive lock shapes, which almost seemed to suggest that someone (or something) was trying to provide the key to the mystery. But what was it?

Fake or genuine, the Alton Barnes circles proved to be big business. Thousands of people flocked to inspect the pattern at close quarters and the shrewd farmer who owned the field made himself a profit by charging visitors an entrance fee!

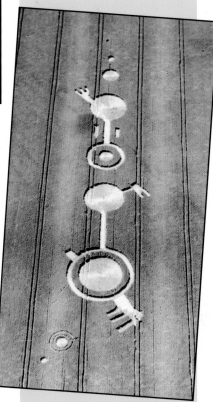

letters of the alphabet.

One of the most complex pictograms to date was found in August 1991. It formed the shape of a mathematical pattern called a Mandelbrot Set, which is known only to scientists, mathematicians, computer buffs... and possibly

intelligent aliens or very smart hoaxers!

HOW CIRCLES APPEAR
The crop is usually flattened in delicately layered swirls, each stalk bent to the ground without killing the plant. Scientists have examined seeds and plants taken from

circles and found that they have altered cell structures and are often malformed in strange ways. Yet the scientists seem unable to explain how these very unusual changes occur.

Are the crop circles just clever hoaxes? Turn the page and find out.

THE HOAXES

Are the mysterious circles simply the work of petty pranksters?

In the summer of 1991, British hoaxers Doug Brewer and Dave Chorley made an astonishing claim. They announced that they were responsible for many of the crop circles that had baffled top scientists.

Newspapers and TV crews gathered to interview the two pranksters, confident that the mystery had finally been solved. But soon, some important questions began to arise. Could two elderly men really have created hundreds of circles all over the country? How did they manage to move around at night without being seen by anyone? And just how did they get into the middle of fields without leaving tracks?

GIVE IT THE BOOT

Another group of hoaxers, calling themselves the Wessex Skeptics, also declared that they were responsible for many of the strange crop circles.

Hoaxers claim that the shapes are made by using planks of wood attached to pieces of string or chains wound around a central pole. Some even figure that the best way is to trample the crop down in a circular shape with nothing more sophisticated than a pair of hefty boots! But none of these methods would have created the beautiful curled, swirled, and layered patterns that the flattened stalks usually leave behind.

WHODUNNIT?

Crop circle experts claim that they can always tell which of the circles are fake – most are more ragged, with lots of broken plant stalks. And farmers usually know when strangers have been walking in their fields. Could the hoaxers really have gotten away with it?

A huge crop pattern in Highland, Kansas, was claimed to be a prank. But someone was taking it

FIELD PHENOMENA

⭐ Crop circles became big news in the 1990s, but it looks as though there may be nothing new about these fascinating field phenomena.

Wood carvings dating back to the late 17th century have been found that seem to show the devil cutting down crops in a circular shape. And later images such as this one, below, show a horned devil being shooed away from "his work" – possibly a crop circle – by a female fieldworker.

But are these images concrete evidence of devilish crop circle connections? It doesn't seem likely – after all, the devil often features strongly in country superstitions and usually takes the blame for anything that can't be readily explained.

seriously – the mysterious government investigators who sealed off the area, tried to hide the circle, and prevented the item from appearing on the local news.

In Grasdorf, Germany, a huge 6,500-square-foot pattern was claimed to be a hoax. But such a vast and precisely detailed example would be difficult to achieve without the hoaxers'

attracting attention.

Some experts on crop circles believe that small whirlpools of air could cause the shapes. But would they be able to make some of the fine detailing seen in so many of these strange phenomena? Or is it possible that crop circles are special signs left behind by visitors from outer space – coded messages that we haven't yet learned to crack?

IN 1991 DAVE CHORLEY AND DOUG BREWER CLAIMED THEY HAD MADE THE CIRCLES.

IT'S ALL A BIG JOKE – WE MADE THE CIRCLES.

AND LOTS OF PEOPLE HAVE BEEN COPYING US.

EXPERTS GATHERED TO CHECK THEIR STORY...

YOU DO IT LIKE THIS, WITH BOARDS AND STRING. WE'VE BEEN DOING IT FOR YEARS!

BUT YOU'RE BREAKING THE STALKS – THAT'S MUCH MORE RAGGED THAN A REAL CIRCLE.

ARE THEY MA BY HOAXERS OR BY FREAK WEATHER CONDITIONS?

OR IS IT A MYSTER ENERGY – MAYBE AN ALIEN SPACEC YOU DECIDE!

Half woman, half fish – but is the amazing mermaid just a myth?

Folk tales from all over the world tell of a race of creatures – half human, half fish – that live at the bottom of the sea. But are these stories just fishy tales?

From head to waist, legend has it that merfolk look just like ordinary humans. But from the waist down, they're said to be covered in scales. Most folklore focuses on the females, mythical maids who sit on rocks, combing their long, golden hair and admiring themselves in mirrors. A couple of centuries ago, every sailor was warned of these malicious sirens who would sing sweetly to passing ships, luring the sailors to their doom on dangerous rocks.

MER-MANIA!

Columbus reported seeing three mermaids on his voyage to America in 1492. But many sightings have also taken place on the Scottish coast. In 1833, six Shetland fishermen apparently caught a mermaid in their nets off the island of Yell. For three hours she howled miserably, until they released her into the sea.

Just three years earlier, in 1830, another mermaid was found off the west coast of Scotland on the island of Benbecula. Locals cutting seaweed had spotted her frolicking in the sea a few days before her body was washed up on the beach. So sure was the local sheriff that she was at least part human that he ordered a shroud and coffin for the poor creature.

MISTAKEN IDENTITY

Nowadays, few scientists take the mermaid theory seriously. It's widely believed that manatees, dugongs, or even dolphins could have been mistaken for mermaids by lonely sailors.

Splash!

▲ *What a mix-up! Would you confuse a manatee with a mermaid?*

27

THE FLYING DUTCHMAN

The ghostly galleon that takes to the high seas on a never-ending voyage

It is March 1939. The beach at False Bay, near Cape Town, South Africa, is packed with sunbathers and swimmers. It is a bright, sunny day and suddenly a huge sailing ship is spotted in the bay. It's under full sail, yet there's not a breath of wind. How can this be?

More than 100 people witnessed the appearance of this ship. Minutes later it vanished. Could this have been the notorious ghostly galleon, the *Flying Dutchman*, said to be cursed to sail the seven seas until the end of time?

The legend began with Hendrik van der Decken, the Dutch skipper of a ship sailing from Holland to the East Indies. The *Flying Dutchman* hit a bad storm around the Cape of Good Hope and the crew begged van der Decken to turn back. He refused, swearing he would round the Cape "or be forever damned." When the vessel finally lost its battle against the elements, van der Decken was doomed to sail his ship until the end of time.

CELEBRITY SPOTTER

Hundreds of sailors claim to have seen the ghost ship. Prince George, later King George V of England, was a midshipman on H.M.S. *Inconstant*. On July 11, 1881, he saw the *Flying Dutchman* off the coast of Australia. Thirteen others in the crew also saw the ship. Rumor and superstition surround most sightings, and this one is no exception. Shortly after the ghost ship's appearance, the very first sailor who caught sight of it dropped dead.

MAYDAY! MAYDAY! Today, sailors believe that an appearance by the *Flying Dutchman* is a sure sign of approaching danger.

THE MYSTERY OF THE MARY CEL

LOOK AT THAT STRANGE SHIP, SIR. SHE'S SAILING VERY BADLY.

ON DECEMBER 5, 1872, THE CREW OF A BRITISH VESSEL, THE *DEI GRATIA*, CAME ACROSS A STRANGE SHIP DRIFTING IN THE ATLANTIC...

When a ship called the was found abandoned discovery raised many intri For a start, there was no sign had mysteriously disappeared Where had they gone? And w deserted a ship that was far fr

The most likely explanation had fled in panic. But what ha scare them? And were the un found on a raft early the next remained of the doomed *Mar*

Do you believe in fairies? Elsie Wright and her cousin Frances Griffiths said they did. In fact, they even found some living at the bottom of Elsie's backyard. And to prove it, they took some amazing pictures.

During the hot summer of 1917, Frances and Elsie took five photographs that stunned the world. They showed the girls playing with their friends near a brook in Cottingley, West Yorkshire, England. Nothing unusual about that, you might think – except these friends turned out to be fairies!

READ ALL ABOUT IT!

Lots of other people believed in the fairies, too – including Sir Arthur Conan Doyle, the famous creator of Sherlock Holmes and a firm believer in the supernatural. Conan Doyle had the photographs tested and declared that they were not fakes. He wrote about the case in *Strand* magazine, complete with "the most astounding photographs ever published." It sold out in days and caused a huge stir all over the country.

CLOSE ENCOUNTERS

Years later, Elsie and Frances admitted that the "fairies" were paper cutouts propped up by hat pins and brooches. Frances said they had faked the photographs because it had proved impossible to photograph the real fairies they had seen in the garden. But Elsie claimed they had originally planned the prank to keep Frances out of trouble for falling into a brook.

Some UFO experts claim that stories of encounters with fairies are so similar to stories of close encounters with aliens that they must be one and the same thing. Perhaps that's why Frances and Elsie thought their flighty fairy friends were out of this world!

FAIRY DIFFICULT!

Can you answer these testing fairy teasers?

1 What is the fairy called in J.M. Barrie's *Peter Pan*?

2 Whose famous fairy godmother told her, "You shall go to the ball!"

3 In Shakespeare's *A Midsummer Night's Dream*, who are the king and queen of the fairies (left)?

Answers on page 32

FAIRY TALES!

Are there fairies in *your* backyard? Capture them on camera and you could become famous!

▲ *Frances (above) and Elsie, (above left) frolic with the fairies in Cottingley, West Yorkshire, England.*

A FUNGI TO BE WITH?

★ Rings of toadstools are known as fairy rings. According to folklore, if you put one foot in the ring you can see the fairies. If you stand with both feet in the ring, the fairies will take you prisoner. There are also tales of people who have spent what seems to have been a night watching fairies dancing in a ring, only to return home to find that 50 years of their lives have passed.

INDEX

ANSWERS TO QUESTIONS ON PAGE 30
1. Tinkerbell **2.** Cinderella **3.** Oberon and Titania